MW00667581

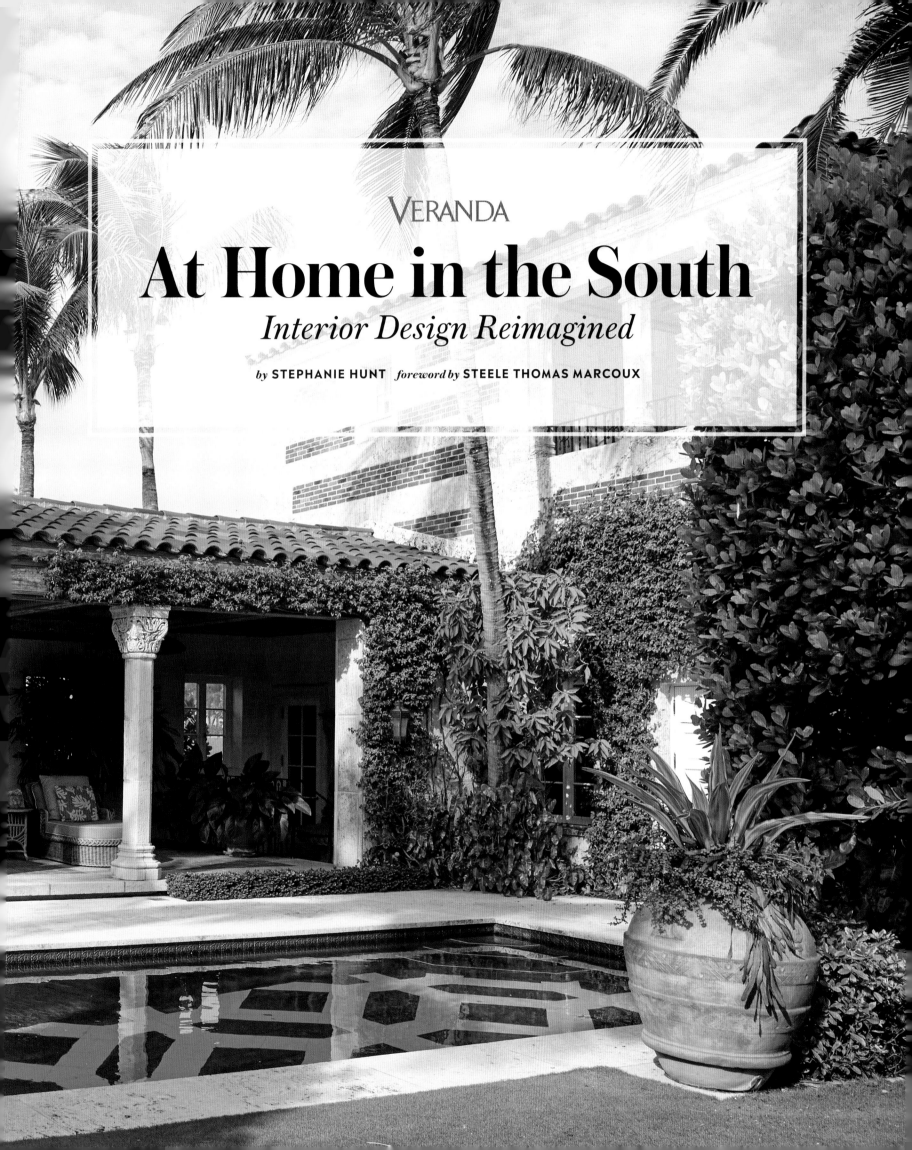

VERANDA

At Home in the South
Interior Design Reimagined

by STEPHANIE HUNT   *foreword by* STEELE THOMAS MARCOUX

CONTENTS

OPPOSITE Cool and classic, with stone floors below and aged timbers above, this Birmingham home exudes country sophistication.

FOREWORD

"BE PRETTY IF YOU CAN, witty if you must, but be gracious if it kills you." So said Elsie de Wolfe, America's first professional decorator and a masterful hostess of rather extravagant parties. But what exactly does it mean to be gracious? At Veranda, this question feels as fundamental to our mission today as it did in 1987, when our founder Lisa Newsom launched the magazine from her home in Atlanta.

During my tenure at the helm of this brand, I've found myself using the word time and again as a way of defining *Veranda's* unique point of view. "Our stories celebrate, and are meant to inspire, gracious living," I've said. Though I didn't give it much thought at the time, I'm sure I was thinking of how being gracious can mean, broadly speaking, living with style, beauty, and luxurious comfort. When it comes to entertaining at home, the art of gracious living becomes a bit more specific: a gracious host is well-mannered, considerate, and accommodating. (Of course, being a gracious host is no easy feat, even though the best of them make it look so, which calls for adding *clever* to the list of required traits.)

Though it may come as a surprise, Lisa never intended for the magazine to be considered "Southern"—that's part of why she eschewed the word in its title. Instead, she sought to shine a light on the art of gracious living: decorating with exceptional taste, entertaining at home with ease, cultivating a passion for flowers and gardens, connecting deeply with nature.

But in our quest for inspiring others on how to be gracious, we find ourselves returning to our own Southern roots time and again. Maybe it's the premium Southerners place on heirlooms and rituals, setting the table with their grandmothers' silver regardless of whether or not company is coming. Perhaps it's the emphasis on home itself, where most Southerners choose to gather with friends and family to break bread, knowing that meals together in a beautiful, welcoming setting are every bit as much about nourishment for our souls as any other kind. It might have something to do with the climate since offering a neighbor a glass of iced tea on the porch could easily be considered a form of survival as it could a hospitable gesture.

No matter the reason, living graciously in every sense of the word—from creating a beautiful, inviting home and being a thoughtful host to extending compassion and kindness to neighbors and strangers alike—defines what it means to be at home in the South.

STEELE THOMAS MARCOUX

OPPOSITE A wickered porch tucked beneath Italianate arches conjures comfort and ease in this Palm Beach home.

INTRODUCTION

FROM ITS START IN ATLANTA, *Veranda* has always been a magazine with Southern roots, even as it has showcased examples of the best home design around the globe. As these pages reveal, the South holds its own as a design mecca, with swoon-worthy style to be found in every corner, along every coast, and in each nook and cranny of the region. To be at home in the South is to cross thresholds of warmth and welcome and to lay claim to a centuries-old legacy of refinement. Mostly though, to be at home here, a land where scars and shadows run deep, is to understand that despite a complicated and often shameful past, the South has always been home to diverse points of view, reflected in a richly diverse, enduringly sophisticated, stereotype-defying aesthetic.

Southern style resists easy categorizing, and certainly defies cliché. There may be magnolias and swooping live oaks gracing a home's exterior, perhaps even sweet tea in the fridge, but inside, design runs the gamut, and always has. Sure, we love our chintz and grandma's handmade quilt, but modernist nods and eclectic palettes are equally at home here too. The one common denominator: an abiding love of beauty.

Today's Southern style is as stunning as ever. Here we peer into a historic Charleston gem freshly re-envisioned for a young family, and marvel over thoughtful details of both a tiny Tennessee log cabin and a tony Texas mansion. From Atlanta to Charlotte, from Palm Beach to Birmingham to Brays Island, the South's top designers are creating such a wide array of work that we chose to organize these chapters not by region or style, but by broader themes—houses designed for entertaining, those that reflect the landscape, homes that are exuberantly over-the-top, and so forth. Wander among them, snoop around, hop from house to house as if you're visiting old neighbors (something Southerners are good at doing).

To be at home in the South is to revel in the fact that home, regardless of its color palette or countertops, is always personal. Southern style is not a thing unto itself, but a mirror, ornate or not, reflecting those who make their lives here. It is classic and genteel, contemporary and edgy. It's both elegantly layered and boldly unpredictable. Whatever else the so-called New South may be, it remains rooted in exceptional taste and is perfectly happy to let beauty speak for itself.

OPPOSITE A symphony of soft lilac blues serenade a sitting area in a New Orleans bedroom.

◆ CHAPTER 1 ◆

A Gracious Welcome

TO THE UNINITIATED, Southern hospitality may seem like a trope, but it is not mere myth. It's more like an urge, a tickle that needs scratching. Though amorphous and, yes, uneven (not every "y'all" comes with a big warm hug), an inkling toward open doors and "come have a seat" is indeed ubiquitous among Southerners. It seems more hardwired than geographic happenstance, as baked into the Southern experience as butter in biscuits.

It's hard to know where this impulse toward graciousness comes from—this "bustling, ineffable hospitality" that Tennessee resident and author Jon Meacham deems "uniquely Southern." But we know it when we see it. It looks like a wide, welcoming front porch. A beckoning foyer. A thoughtfully stocked bar and lavishly set dining table. A sweet reading nook. It's a get-comfy formal living room that "surrenders every iota of stuffiness," as Alabama-based designer Caroline Gidiere says.

In Nashville, the Meachams indulge their "instinct for convening" in a 1930s Georgian Revival designed by Brockschmidt & Coleman with "a generous shot of soul" and ample room for gathering friends around the table. Near Birmingham, designer Mark D. Sikes uses inviting, effusive color to give "Southern gentility a youthful edge" in a midcentury home embraced for its quirks and imperfections. And in rural Georgia, designer Keith Robinson welcomes guests for casual garden dining at his farmhouse.

Like electronic airport signs spelling out "welcome" in multiple languages, there are many ways to create inviting spaces—none exclusive to the South. Here, however, the vernacular of hospitality has a distinctly Southern accent, and it says more than just "come in." As Jon Meacham notes, "hospitality is an outward and visible sign of the inward and invisible virtues of grace, generosity, even love." The door is open.

LEFT Painted brickwork gives the home a look more in line with its 1920s neighbors. In lieu of typical black shutters, Gidiere chose to match the shade to the house for a fresh touch. Various garden nooks extend the home's entertaining space.

PAGES 10-11 Caroline Gidiere's love of symmetry and pattern makes her Birmingham living room a warm and inviting space.

Alabama Exuberance

◆ ◆ ◆

Lawyer-turned-designer Caroline Gidiere embraces
traditional Georgian style with unabashed verve.

LEFT Pastel purples and blues are punctuated by vivid orange in this combo den and breakfast area off the kitchen. "I love timeless rooms but exuberant pattern and color," Gidiere says.

RIGHT French doors invite in abundant natural light, "the best thing you can have in a house," says architect James F. Carter. The living room welcomes a happy mix: Ruffled floral slipcovered sofas fraternize effortlessly with filigreed Kentian consoles and a quieter games table and chairs from the Paris Flea Market.

BELOW Glossy hot-orange millwork adds levity and sizzle to the bar's ultra-traditional built-in cabinetry stained chocolate brown.

> " I love timeless rooms but exuberant pattern and color. "

◇◇◇

CAROLINE GIDIERE,
DESIGNER

PAGE 14 Mountain Brook, Alabama, boasts many English-style homes from the 1920s and 1930s, and while this was a new construction, Gidiere and Carter ensured it fit in, with classic elements like Greek key motif molding summoning late Georgian/Regency influences. A cheerful entry of understated simplicity announces, "Come on in."

PAGE 15 Thanks to parents who dragged her to Colonial Williamsburg each summer, Gidiere fully owns her traditional tastes. "I wanted to do a riff on the George Wythe house," she says of her Williamsburg favorite. Here hand-painted de Gournay wallpaper offsets an antique sideboard, creating the "majestic simplicity" the designer loves.

LEFT Gidiere finds that layering pattern upon pattern—florals, ikat, a stripe rug and a lush upholstered sleigh bed—ironically creates a calming effect.

BELOW Various garden nooks make al fresco entertaining a delight.

LEFT Romantic English floral wallpaper and curtains envelop a spacious and sunny guest bedroom. Gidiere found vintage quilts from a Provence market for the four-poster beds.

Gathered 'Round

◆◆◆

Jon and Keith Meacham don't need
an excuse to host friends in their 1930s Nashville
Georgian. "We celebrate, just because."

Jon

LEFT Fresh flowers on the table, and atop fresh shortbread cookies, make for artful hosting. The vintage plateware is from Keith Meacham's collection.

RIGHT Lush silk curtains frame the bar, where high-ball glasses and goblets from Reed & Company, Keith Meacham's tableware and décor company founded with her late friend Julia Reed, are ready for liquid conviviality.

PAGE 20 The Meachams gravitated back South after 17 years in New York, lured by "dogs and trees," Jon says, but also a slower pace and more room to entertain. Designers Bill Brockschmidt and Courtney Coleman helped them restore a crumbling 1930s Georgian Revival, gilding the dining room in a gold saffron, reminiscent of the chrome yellow of Monticello (fitting for a presidential historian). A 19th-century Italian chandelier adds old-world elegance and fun contrast to the spunky geometric entryway wallcovering.

PAGE 21 Place cards and a gorgeous table setting make guests feel special, even if it's a small gathering. Here peach, pink, and ivory roses complement the table's vibrant jewel tones.

> **❝** One thing remains unchanged from the parties of our childhood—the bustling and ineffable hospitality that seemed then, and still does, uniquely Southern. **❞**

◇◇◇

JON MEACHAM, AUTHOR AND HOMEOWNER

Farm to Table in Georgia

◆ ◆ ◆

Event designer Keith Robinson savors the alfresco pleasures of his rural Georgia farmhouse and gardens.

LEFT Robinson welcomed the challenge of shoring up a sadly sagging circa 1841 farmhouse on 35 rolling acres in Georgia's Chattahoochee Hills. The bones of the formal boxwood gardens, originally planned by famed horticulturalist Prosper Berckmans, still frame the house, outlining an inviting entertaining space.

ABOVE Four different vegetable gardens are conveniently located right outside Robinson's kitchen, where he harvests lettuces, radishes, herbs, and other goodies for an undeniably fresh meal. Robinson uses his home-grown produce in his catering business as well.

LEFT The farmhouse was once the main house of a 10,000-acre cattle and cotton plantation that spanned five counties and included a foundry and general store. Robinson has undertaken its complete restoration, repurposing materials found on-site, including cedar planks found in a barn that he made into kitchen shelves.

ABOVE "Using fine things in the garden creates magic," says Robinson, who pairs antique china and silver with lilac linens and a chocolaty floral motif tablecloth.

LEFT Confessing to an "obsession" with tableware, Robinson has a collection of 800-some vintage and antique china pieces. He comes by it naturally— "I grew up in a family that set a beautiful table every Sunday," he says.

RIGHT The shade (and fragrance) of a climbing rose trellis offers another inviting location for a late lunch. Wide garden paths are ideal for entertaining—"it's beautiful and dramatic," says Robinson.

Spirit Restored

◆ ◆ ◆

Designer Mark D. Sikes infuses a mix of joyful
gentility and youthful esprit into this Alabama beauty,
enhancing its old quirks with bright color.

LEFT Set on nine acres within Birmingham city limits, this 1950s-era home's intact architectural elements appealed to the owner's nostalgia. In lieu of starting over, she tasked California-based designer Mark Sikes (whom she'd met at a Birmingham design show) with adding lively flair that honored its unique features and pastoral charm. The owners' flock of Finnsheep graze outside.

RIGHT Sikes chose zingy yellows and greens, colors that he says are the "least buttoned-up" and take the edge off formal spaces. A hand-painted Gracie wallpaper blooms in the dining room, while upholstered chairs echo the entryway pattern.

RIGHT A bold entry hall wallcovering sets a lighthearted tone right off the bat, creating a cheerful background for an ornate gilt mirror and antique settee.

PAGE 28-29 In the formal living room, a geometric abaca rug sets the tone for pattern play of ikat mixed with florals and stripes, while sunny yellow walls imbue exuberance and energy to the traditional decor.

LEFT Serene soft blues and creams are layered in the primary bedroom, where an upholstered Highland House bed takes center stage.

RIGHT On the upstairs landing, a boisterous blue mash-up of patterns—checks, florals, and stripes—is surprisingly soothing thanks to a restricted palette.

BELOW Sikes embraces the spirited juxtaposition of young and old, pairing patinaed furnishings with updated fabrics. In this guest room, the old-school romance of florals feels like a comforting throw-back to grandma's house.

> **"** It's as if this house says 'hello' when you walk in, it tells you a story, then it sings to you. And when you leave, you feel loved. **"**

◇◇◇

MARK D. SIKES, DESIGNER

CHAPTER 2

Lure of Landscape

THE SOUTH, BY THE VERY NATURE of the term, is geography. It is the Blue Ridge and the bayou, Low Country marshes, and grassy meadow piedmonts. It is Florida palm trees and Carolina pine forests, with vast stretches of tobacco fields and trout-filled rivers and lakes in between. Just as land and landscape define the region, so too the South's best designers and architects today give an essential nod if not a reverent bow to terrain and natural beauty. They understand what writer Rebecca Solnit suggests: "When you give yourself to places, they give you yourself back."

In the South, porches and patios are designed with as much care as living rooms and kitchens. These outdoor spaces, where the afternoon breeze carries hints of magnolia and evenings hum with cricket songs, are where life happens. Where cocktail glasses clink and kids chase fireflies and a worn-out puppy flops by your feet. The outside is welcomed inside too, with interior palettes of earth and sky, with textures of sea grass and wood grain.

These homes are odes to their environs. In sunny Palm Beach, designer Phoebe Howard embraces flamingos and palm fronds with abandon, while in rural Tennessee, designer Tammy Connor gives rustic a handsome, refined touch. With ample windows and minimalist flair, a North Carolina lake house by designer Cliff Fong blurs the boundaries between outdoors and in, while designer Beth Webb on Brays Island, South Carolina, is inspired by the moss-draped serenity of her sea island surroundings. A wild meadow in the rolling hills of Alabama cradles the home of designer Melanie Pounds's mother and stepfather, where Pounds and architect Paul Bates take their cues from the raw pureness of its bucolic setting.

"Sense of place" is a phrase typically bandied about in Southern literary salons, but what William Faulkner and Eudora Welty did so masterfully on the page, today's Southern style-makers do in three dimensions. Theirs is a dialogue between land and shelter and how they hold, shape, comfort, and inspire us. It's an ongoing tale of memory and imagination, of wind and water, pattern, patina, and, always, place.

LEFT Allées of grand live oaks add drama to the Southern landscape.

PAGE 34-35 Nature sets a relaxed pace on Brays Island, where moss-cloaked trees flank open pastures.

Sea Island Idyll

◆ ◆ ◆

Atlanta-based designer Beth Webb embraces
the natural beauty of South Carolina's Brays Island
in a small cottage full of elegant details.

> **"** I think now more than ever we're all realizing how little we really need, especially when nature is the true sanctuary. **"**

⬦⬦⬦

BETH WEBB, DESIGNER

ABOVE Architect Peter Block used aged clinker bricks with custom mortar, giving a nod to the Low Country vernacular.

PAGE 38-39 English country cottage meets Low Country sportsman lodge, thanks to Block's architectural genius. He's a "master of the new old house," says Webb of this home nestled among old oaks and horse paddocks.

RIGHT "It's like sleeping under a tent, which is fitting out in the country," says Webb of the sloping ceiling covered in wood-grain woven abaca wallcovering.

OPPOSITE A small footprint for this cozy sea island "lodge" necessitated open living spaces that "flow together graciously," says Block, who introduced verticality with tall windows framing the pastoral views. "Nothing feels contained or compressed," he says.

ABOVE Magnolia branches, that iconic Southern greenery, grace an early 20th-century copper cachepot atop an antique French walnut buffet.

LEFT Savannah-based muralist Bob Christian captures the mercurial beauty of Brays Island in this stunning dining room backdrop. Reclaimed white oak beams and a Belgian blue stone floor add earthy elements.

LEFT Soaring windows flood the galley kitchen with dappled light, giving it a "non-kitchen feel, a space that looks more like a sun-splashed garden," says Webb, who used natural materials like custom millwork out of rift-cut white oak.

ABOVE Spring, fall, and winter are ideal for outdoor dining along the South Carolina coast. A swooping gable roof like that found in English country houses mimics the dramatic drape of limbs on nearby grand live oaks.

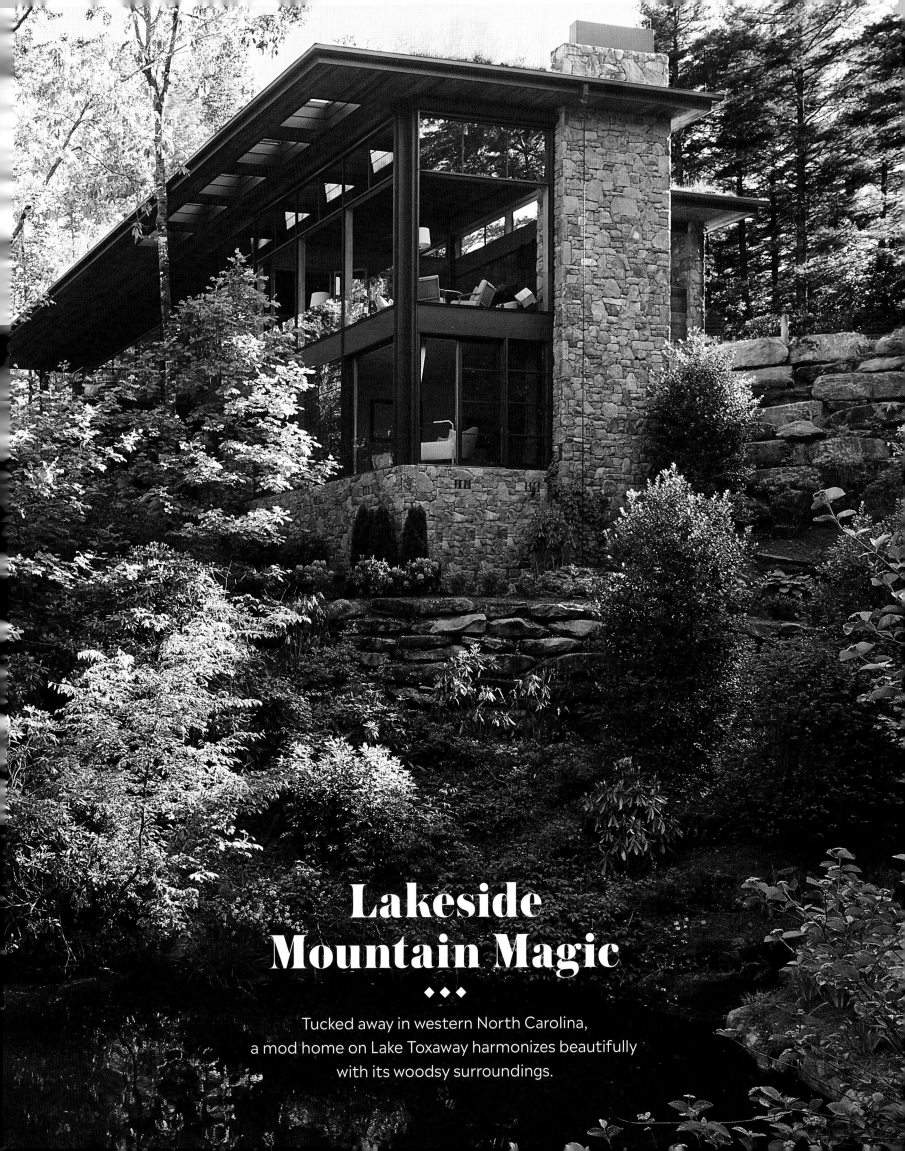

Lakeside Mountain Magic

...

Tucked away in western North Carolina,
a mod home on Lake Toxaway harmonizes beautifully
with its woodsy surroundings.

RIGHT Stonework abounds, fully integrating the pathway from the entrance to the lakeside porch and garden with the landscape.

PAGE 46-47 "There is something amazingly relaxing about being 100 percent surrounded by nature. There's comfort in the landscape," says architect Al Platt.

LEFT For this Lake Toxaway retreat, designer Cliff Fong selected low-profile furniture upholstered in muted, neutral fabrics. "I didn't really want anything to pull focus from the view or get lost in the view," the Los Angeles–based designer says. Retractable screens immerse this sitting room into the mountain landscape.

RIGHT The great room includes something for everyone, from a rousing game of billiards on the custom pool table, to cocktails from the bookshelf bar.

> **"** The last thing the owner wanted was a super-slick, fancy house. It was essential to create something harmonious to the mountains. **"**

◇◇◇

CLIFF FONG, DESIGNER

ABOVE Natural materials, including reclaimed brushed hemlock ceiling cladding, white oak millwork, and granite for the stone fireplace, all sourced from within a one-hour radius of this North Carolina mountain home, underscore the home's kinship with the landscape.

RIGHT A buffet of windows surrounded by Juno limestone backsplash and counters highlights this kitchen's woodsy flavor, starring custom-designed cabinetry in the spirit of midcentury woodworker George Nakashima.

RIGHT Whispering neutrals and gentle, layered textures create a sense of calm in this treehouse-like guest bedroom.

BELOW Thanks to a sunken soaking tub by a sliding glass window that opens fully to the lake breeze, being submerged in nature is sheer luxury.

LEFT A terrace fireplace radiates warmth and coziness outdoors, featuring stone from a nearby quarry. Vladimir Kagan swivel chairs keep the hearthside comfy, with mantel artwork by Nobuo Sekine.

RIGHT Lake breeze? Yes, please! Ample outdoor spaces invite plein air entertaining, relaxing or catching your breath, and a breeze after a day out boating, waterskiing, or paddleboarding.

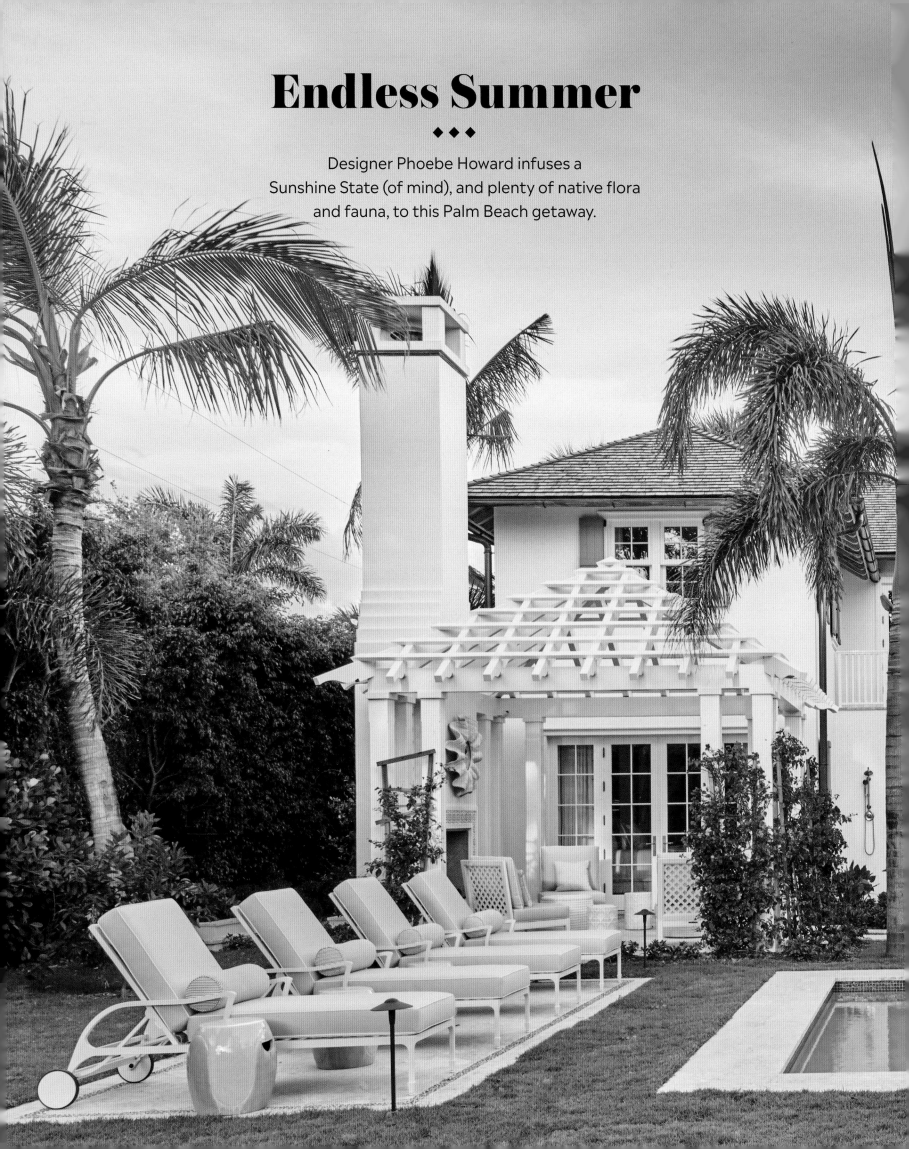

Endless Summer

◆ ◆ ◆

Designer Phoebe Howard infuses a
Sunshine State (of mind), and plenty of native flora
and fauna, to this Palm Beach getaway.

LEFT Classic blue and white is a Southern style staple, especially by the coast where it amplifies sea and sky. With cheerful stripes and a mix of warm-weather textures, Howard complies with her client's request: "She wanted the colors you see in Palm Beach—the flora, the sea, the sky."

RIGHT No-fail geraniums add a burst of color to this blue and white feast, where a striped rug plays well with Katie Leede & Company's fresh take on a vintage-style wallpaper pattern. A Tole palm tree serves as a sculptural focal point.

RIGHT A crisp all-white kitchen keeps things cool in the South's warm climate, and contrasts with the home's colorful spaces.

PAGE 54-55 Sunshine, warmth, and happy, chill vibes set the tone for this vacation home that Jacksonville-based Howard designed for a Midwest couple seeking a winter thaw.

LEFT Seashells and sea horses make for sweet Florida dreams in this guest bedroom, featuring a headboard covered in citrusy lime, a bright but earthy hue that juxtaposes well with the grasscloth wallcovering.

BELOW Flamingos in an artful graphic wallpaper pay homage to a familiar Florida neighbor, while Howard added simple café curtains and an antique chair in checked fabric to balance the busy pattern.

LEFT Bright corals shine in the main bedroom, with windows dressed in a China Seas print, and a whisper-of-pink wall covering gives the sense that one might be cuddled inside a whelk shell.

ABOVE Here Howard brings the outdoors in, literally, with a detail-rich trellis ceiling and walls and wicker chair and ottoman. Natural textures abound in the woven grass rug and coffee table.

RIGHT Nothing says Florida like a well-appointed poolside pergola. Lucky guests get easy access to this one, connecting the guest suite to the pool and back lawn. Howard chose chairs by McKinnon and Harris to complement the trellis work.

Rustic Retreat

••••

In a small log cabin in Sewanee, Tennessee, designer
Tammy Connor goes big on creature comforts.

LEFT Nostalgia meets high performance in this forest green galley kitchen featuring an old school farm sink and capable Viking range. Connor opted for English antiques–"French would have felt too sweet," she says–including this table surrounded by antique rattan chairs.

RIGHT In a sleeping loft, curtained rope beds are tucked under the eaves for a magical privacy. A hunter's horn and trophy antlers feel like they've been there for centuries.

BELOW An antique poster bed dressed in Classic Cloth linen harmonizes with the cabin's in-the-forest vibe, while the chair in a traditional Zoffany plaid adds color. "I wanted it to feel like an enveloping, masculine old cabin that has been updated," says Connor.

PAGE 62 A 1,200-square-foot woodsy Tennessee cabin lives large, thanks to refined detail by Birmingham-based architect James F. Carter, who flanked the vaulted living room ceiling in reclaimed wood from an old barn. Hand-hewn timbers circa 1840 give the log cabin authentic flavor, while Connor, also based in Birmingham, selected traditional furnishings for low-key comfort.

PAGE 63 When so much time is spent enjoying the great outdoors, interior spaces need not be large. Here a loft bedroom accommodates guests, and a ladder subs in for stairs. Connor selected crewel pillows and a rustic coffee table that are homey yet handsome.

Meadow Lark

◆◆◆

In Mountain Brook, Alabama, architect Paul Bates
and designer Melanie Pounds collaborate
on a classic charmer set in a field of dreams.

“ We focused on details that would give the home
a sense of age, but in a fresh way. ”

◇◇◇

MELANIE POUNDS, DESIGNER

PAGE 66-67 Bates designed a home that folds into its surrounding rolling fields. "They wanted the house to feel rambling and unplanned. They love the romance and pureness of that," he says of the owners' desires for their home.

LEFT Elegance is the art of simplicity: Witness silver goblets pairing perfectly with a spray of meadow wildflowers. A cozy banquette accompanied by custom ivory leather stools basks in the breakfast nook's natural light.

BELOW Working with architect Paul Bates, Pounds designed a centerpiece white oak and marble kitchen that leads into a blue-green sitting room with breakfast nook, seamlessly blending living and working spaces, and serving up lovely landscape views.

ABOVE Planted in a meandering wild meadow near Birmingham, Alabama, this new home evokes romance and rootedness to the land. With antique white-oak beams, limestone floors, and steel-cased windows framing the pastoral view, earthy materials are softened by lush fabrics and finishes. A landscape diptych by Michael Dines graces a carved European mantel.

RIGHT "Serene neutrals draw the eye outside," says Pounds, who layered lush cream and beige linens to make the primary bedroom a peaceful haven. French doors lead to the adjacent flower garden.

BELOW Morning coffee or an evening pour of bourbon? Either (or both) would be ideal for this antique wingback perch in the "keeping room," as the owners call this all-purpose room off the kitchen, where Pounds combines earthy tones with luxurious sateen and a dazzling sunburst mirror.

LEFT In Pounds's take on it, classic Southern style welcomes the unexpected, like a formal chandelier gracing a Waterworks soaking tub. Handsome oak paneling gives this bathroom an old-world elegance.

RIGHT Louvered doors lead to a lovely loggia, where shade beckons and outdoor breezes refresh. The stone exterior and pebble courtyard help marry the exterior with the landscape.

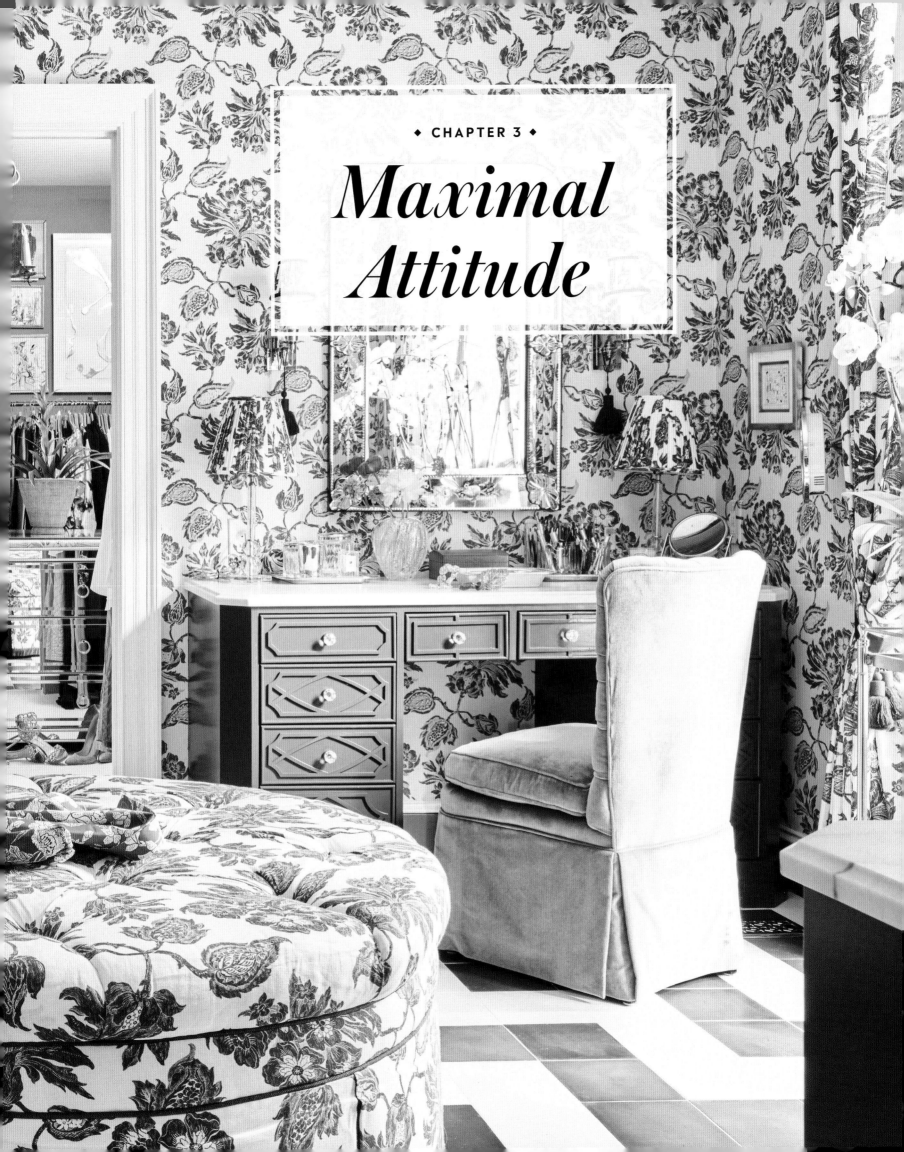

• CHAPTER 3 •

Maximal Attitude

LEFT Designer Danielle
Rollins plays up
sumptuous symmetry
atop an antique chest.
Peachy pinks and
greens parlay a feminine
playfulness.

PAGES 72-73 Wonder
Woman (Lynda Carter
photo) sets an intrepid
tone in Rollins's
bathroom, where
Thibault-covered walls
and upholstery further
pump up a power
attitude.

SOMETIMES MORE ISN'T MORE. It's just right. As with a talented chef who amplifies spice and flavor, for a gifted designer there's no such thing as too much pattern or color. In the South, bigness is revered—this is the land of Dolly Parton and fiery jambalaya, after all, and over-the-top is often just how we like it. Not for the sake of being showy, but because it's authentic.

The proportion and scale of many Southern homes invites one to turn up the volume. Plus, sometimes, age simply has its advantages, and older homes, like those featured here, are much like elder adults—they're ready to be bold and throw caution to the wind. When reinvigorating her 18th-century single house, Charleston-based designer Ceara Donnelley playfully intuited that restraint is often best restrained, so she lacquered a hyphen between formal rooms in electric chartreuse. As she and the other designers included here demonstrate, design taken to the max renders maximal delight.

For Cathy Kincaid in Dallas, showcasing a client's vast porcelain collection could have resulted in platter overload. Instead, she discovers, "the more you add, the less busy it can seem." Similarly, the decidedly not meek Danielle Rollins of Atlanta fully embraces dramatic wallcoverings layered with energetic fabrics and art in her 1970s-era Georgian. "The vibrancy of a background color or pattern can make your art come alive," she says. In New Orleans, Jane Scott Hodges revels in a "decorating adventure" that pulls out all the stops, along with all the silks and luxurious embroidered linens.

Confidence, attitude, big ol' heaping servings of Southern exuberance. Bring it on.

Bold Reboot

⬩⬩⬩

Atlanta-based designer and author
Danielle Rollins doesn't hold back, turning a
1930s Georgian into a showcase of wow.

PAGE 76-77 A curated rainbow of blue, tobacco, coral, and off-white unites an explosion of patterns in the living room. "If you have Picassos, then you can have a white wall," says Rollins, who hung a favorite Kelly O'Neal abstract over the stippled azure scrolls of Toile de Nantes wallpaper.

LEFT A geometric floor spices up Rollins's blue and white kitchen, but no subdued blue here—peacock blue, her favorite color. Brass accents on the custom hood, the Circa Lighting drum pendants, and cabinet hardware add extra flavor.

ABOVE Rollins designed the breakfast room's woven hyacinth dining chairs, which complement the vintage wicker chest. Blue and white ginger jar lamps are timeless, and pop against the vivid blue walls.

LEFT A spirited upholstered bar, tufted and topped in leather, plays well with zingy oranges and bold blue.

> **“If you buy good pieces that you love, you're always going to find a place for them.”**

◇◇◇

DANIELLE ROLLINS, DESIGNER AND HOMEOWNER

LEFT In the dining room, a grounding green is crowned with an apricot-lacquered ceiling that casts a flattering glow. Rollins dresses her table surrounded by antique Italian chairs in an Oscar de la Renta tablecloth, for an easy (and changeable) touch of pizzazz.

ABOVE "If you don't like something, you can always change it," Rollins says—advice she learned from designer Miles Redd. By that token, her bedroom sitting area is unlikely to change. A bouquet of Lee Jofa chintz, leopard print, fanciful trellis walls, and ice-blue satin, it's "all the things I love."

PAGES 82-83 Rollins's canopy bed takes satin and chintz, literally, over the top.

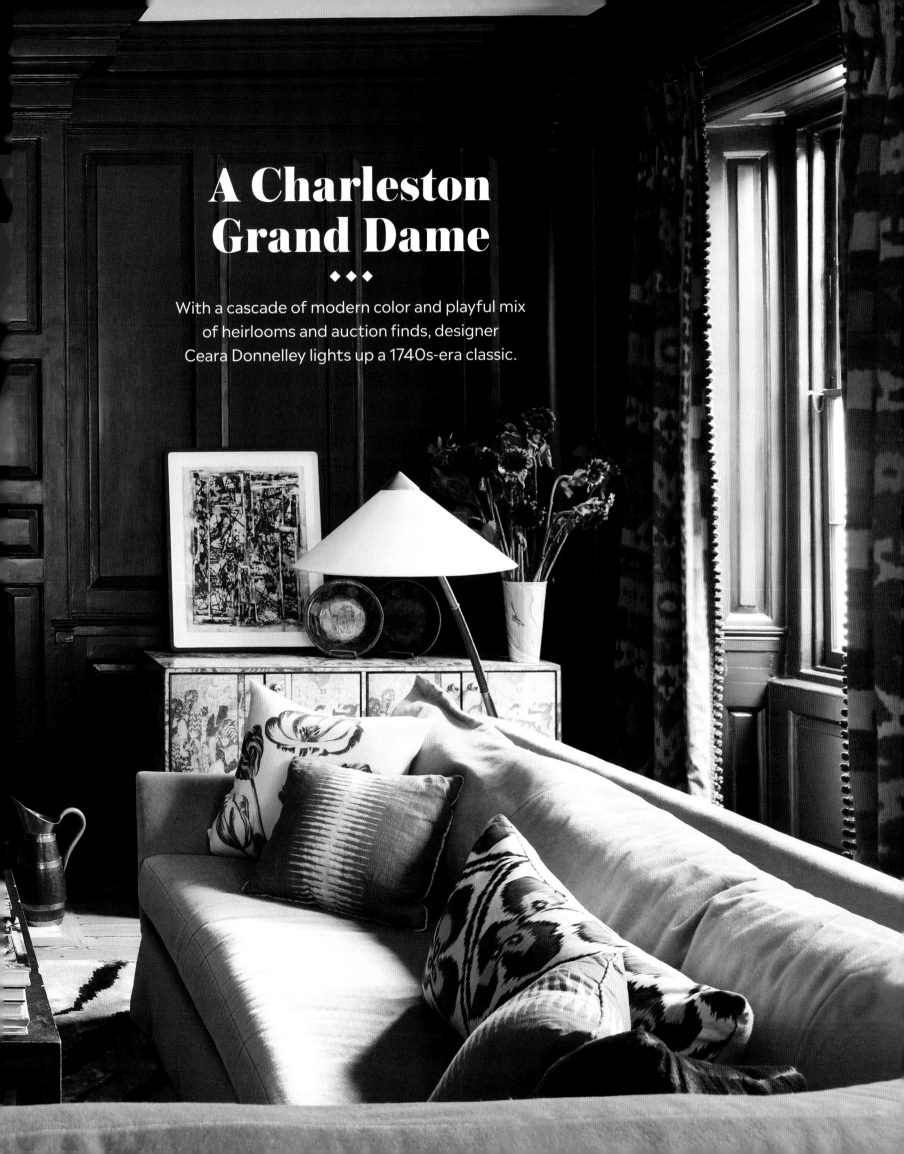

A Charleston Grand Dame

◆ ◆ ◆

With a cascade of modern color and playful mix of heirlooms and auction finds, designer Ceara Donnelley lights up a 1740s-era classic.

LEFT The stucco exterior stayed a salmony terra-cotta per Charleston's historic district guidelines, but Donnelley added a pool and garden. Though the house fronts tourist-heavy and bustling Rainbow Row, the private garden is a tucked-away retreat.

RIGHT Family heirlooms, like a chinoiserie armoire and prints from her father's art collection, anchor the living room, where a 1920s gilt palm chandelier adds dazzle. "My design is driven by a deeply felt idea of home and a spirit of playful experimentation," Donnelley says.

RIGHT Small details, like the tassel fringe drapery trim, add drama and intrigue, luring the eye into the upstairs sitting room, where a Paul McCobb daybed doubles as overflow guest space.

PAGES 84-85 Donnelley embraced zesty color to bring fresh verve to her 18th-century Charleston home. "I loved that the original interiors were intact and hadn't been updated since the 1970s, giving me great raw material for making my own imprint," says Donnelley, who painted the library paneling a deep plum. A pale lavender mohair sofa and jazzy patterned pillows and chairs juxtapose with the moody walls.

LEFT Dining room paneling in robin's egg blue—a hue borrowed from the nearby historic Drayton Hall—pops against white loop chairs.

ABOVE "I love the unexpected, whether a supercharged color or an interesting shape," says Donnelley, who unleashed a jolt of chartreuse to the hyphen connecting the dining room and butler's pantry.

ABOVE A serpent lamp stands guard over a velvet-covered chaise in a cozy corner of the master bedroom.

RIGHT Despite lush linens and elegant touches, including a 1960s French Baguès-style ship chandelier, the designer's bedroom—an homage to her grandmother's signature yellow—is where Donnelley, her kids, and cats often hang out. Which is why the silk brocade she adores is atop the canopy tester—"where it's kid- and cat-safe."

Dallas Tour de Force

❖ ❖ ❖

A historic Spanish Colonial comes to life
thanks to designer Cathy Kincaid's sure hand,
sublime palette, and plenty of porcelain.

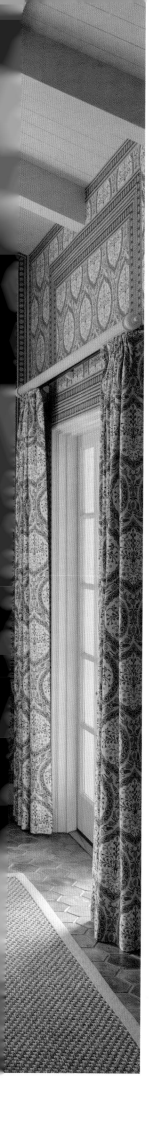

LEFT Indulging in abundant pattern allows Kincaid to set a stage so architectural gems, like this fireplace, stand out. "They really understood the sensibility of the house," she says of the homeowners' thoughtful renovation.

ABOVE Kincaid used a pair of antique confessional doors inset with a transom made from an old Indian table to frame the dining room. The homeowner's extensive porcelain collection sets the blue and white palette, amplified by Portuguese tile wainscoting.

PAGES 92-93 Lavender gray walls create a neutral shell for patterns and colors. Antique textiles and painted furniture in soft red, violet, and gold feel gentle and worn-in, while Kincaid arranged different seating areas to make the spacious room warm and inviting.

LEFT A wall of antiqued mirror frames a fireplace, creating a luminous foyer and a lovely showcase for white porcelain.

RIGHT A to-the-studs renovation of this 1930s-era home restored all windows to their original glory. Kincaid chose a mod Ann Sacks tile for the sunroom floor. "The colors and patterns talk to each other rather than collide. The more you add, the less busy it can seem," she says.

RIGHT Boxwood parterres offer various points of entry to the front garden, adding geometric contrast to the curvy Spanish-influenced architecture.

PAGES 98-99 Creamy beiges and dreamy blues create softness in the light-filled bedroom. A custom poster bed is dressed in Leontine Linens, while painted antique chairs and a custom chandelier are detail-rich.

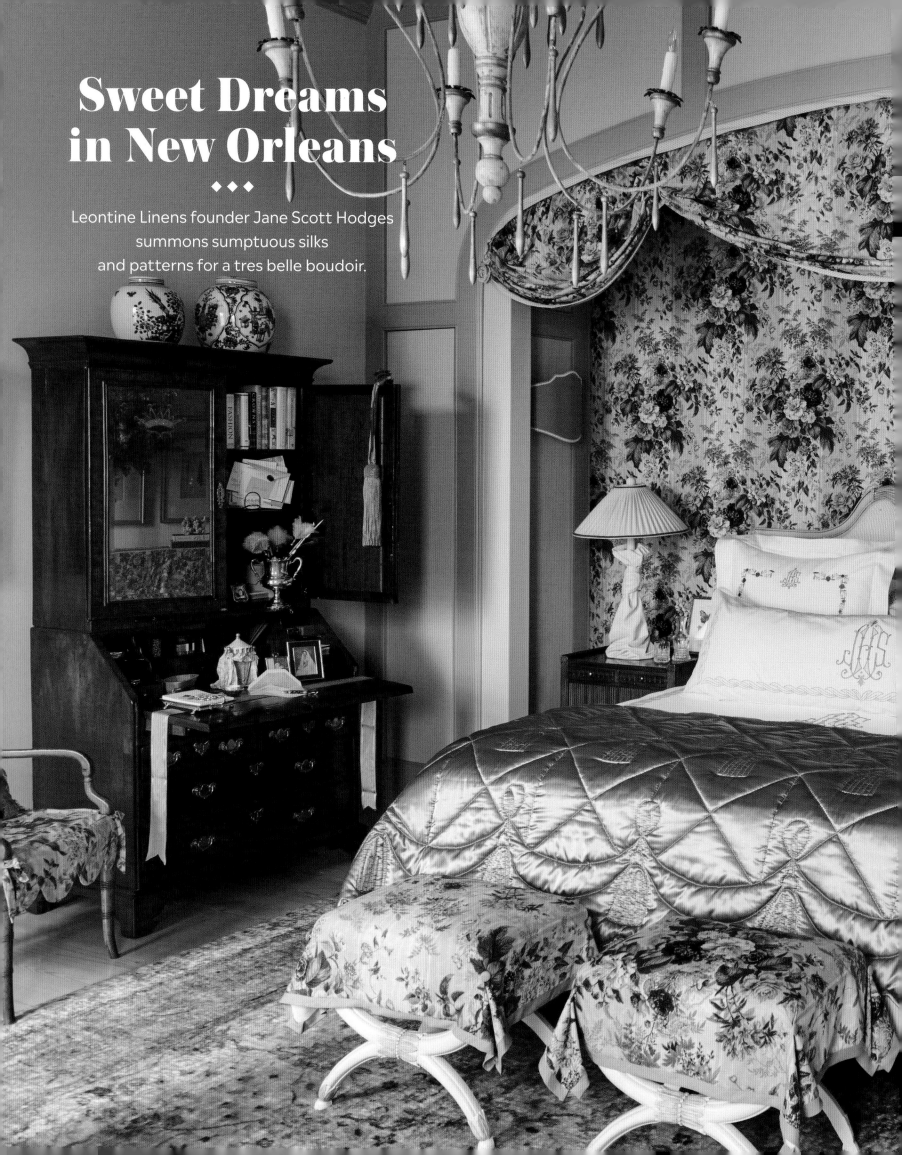

Sweet Dreams in New Orleans

❖❖❖

Leontine Linens founder Jane Scott Hodges
summons sumptuous silks
and patterns for a tres belle boudoir.

PAGES 100-101 Hodges's bed alcove is draped with 30 yards of Pierre Frey's Mortefontaine fabric, a Second Empire floral designed in the same era as her 1830s home. "The pattern had all the hidden subtleties of color we wanted. The faint aqua stripe of the sea and the light and dark blues of the sky—they were all there," the linen designer says.

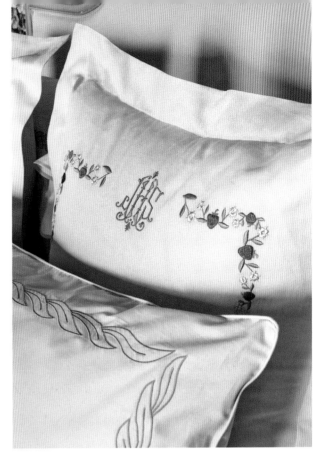

ABOVE Fine linens with personal monograms are a Southern statement of refined class and taste.

BELOW The dying art of the handwritten note is alive and well in well-mannered Southern households like Hodges's—thus a boudoir secretary stocked with writing accoutrements and other treasures.

LEFT Hodges added custom-milled lattice to existing wall paneling— an ode to New Orleans's enchanting garden rooms. In lieu of curtains for the bath's arch, a graceful pelmet with grosgrain appliqué highlights the Calacatta marble veining.

ABOVE An upholstered closet in the bedroom's entry vestibule holds Hodges's exquisitely organized bedding. Her method: After a good ironing, a matching flat sheet and pillow sham are folded to display their embroidery, then tied to a linen board.

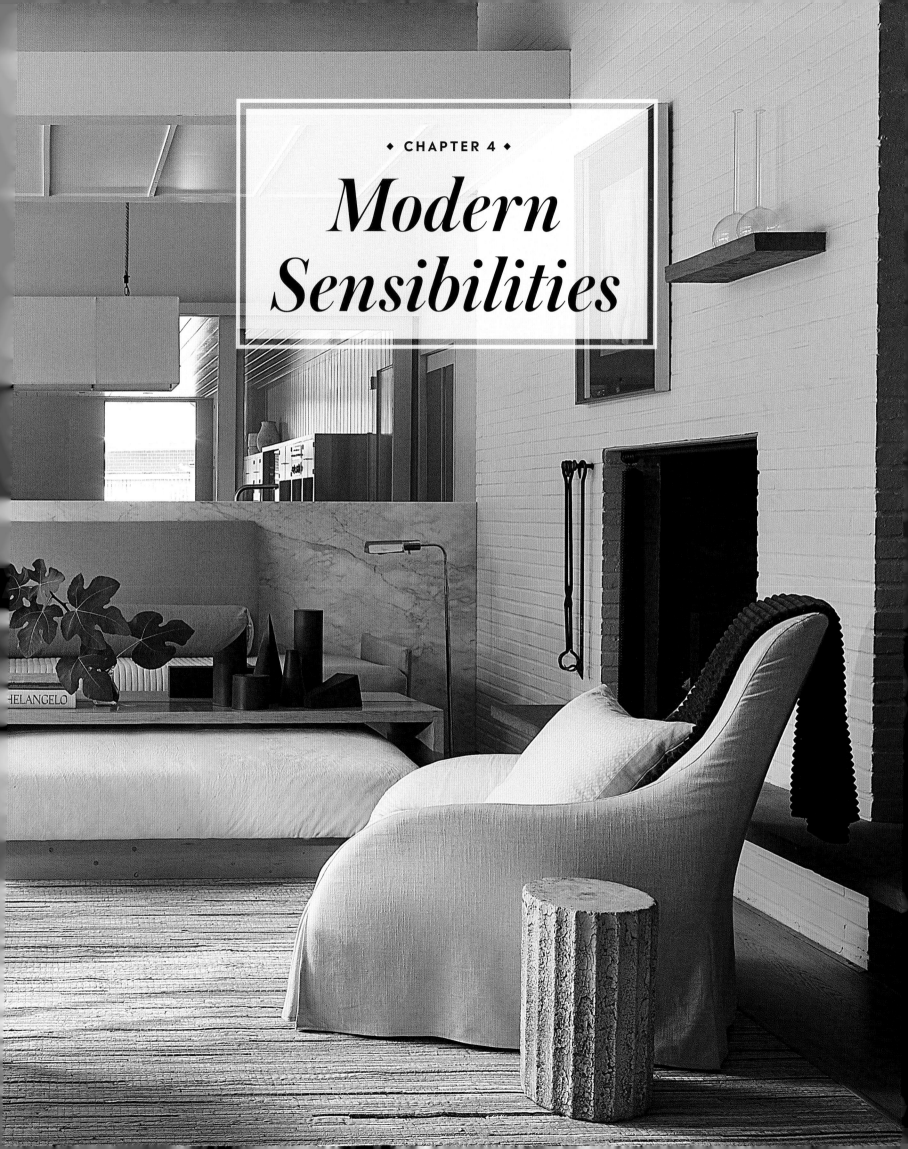

CHAPTER 4

Modern Sensibilities

T RADITION ISN'T GOING ANYWHERE in a region where the past, as Faulkner famously claimed, "is not even past." Even so, some of the South's top architects and designers continually add fresh, modern takes on traditional forms, sometimes eschewing "tradition" altogether. In urban neighborhoods and on quiet back roads, contemporary homes politely mingle among the South's more stayed and storied manses. The mellow lines of a midcentury rambler gently meld with the well-starched and primly shuttered Georgians in Buckhead and Dallas. Design is a time-machine marvel. Even 18th- and 19th-century relics get rejuvenated by svelte interiors dressed in spare, modern sensuousness.

In Charlotte, architect Ken Pursley embraced the "quiet genius of modern architecture" because he wanted a house he could learn from, a space that engaged him in "an ongoing dialogue between old and new." For Bobby McAlpine in Atlanta, designing an unapologetically mod abode entails inviting his home's "soulful qualities to be expressed without makeup and embellishment." Atlanta-based designer Meredith McBrearty ups the suburban swagger of a Dallas midcentury gem, using natural materials in a sophisticated, modern way.

In design studios and homes across the South, the past and present, and indeed the future, chatter nonstop, as new voices with fresh edginess enliven the discourse. As designer Richard Hallberg discovered in Nashville, where he filled a Graceland-esque white-columned mansion with artfully modern interiors, juxtaposition between the expected and unexpected, deepens the story. "I love how objects so different can have a conversation," he says. Traditional or contemporary, stately white columns or blocky white tower—it makes little matter, notes Pursley, for "it's not how a building looks from the outside but how it feels on the inside that merits its worth."

LEFT Natural light, bold shapes, and a soothing earthiness ground this midcentury living room.

PAGE 104-105 This 1950s-era Saul Edelbaum–designed home was on the state preservation office's endangered list before architect and designer Ken Pursley rescued it. In the living room, he separates the seating area from an open kitchen with a Calacatta marble partition, which doubles as a back-drop showcasing the custom-sofa wedding gift from friend and colleague Bobby McAlpine.

Midcentury Masterpiece

••••

North Carolina architect Ken Pursley unlocks the
wit and wisdom within his 1950s iconic Charlotte home.

JULIUS SHULMAN

RIGHT Pursley likes the energy infusion that comes from pulling the kitchen into the social realm. "I call this the 'Japanese Steakhouse' plan," he says, where cook and guests can interact, but cleanup happens "backstage" in the pantry concealed by a glass-and-vinyl-clad pivot.

BELOW Dark bronze plaster walls are designed to "fall into shadow," says Pursley, allowing the original amber-shellacked oak cabinetry to shine.

ABOVE Original white-oak dowels create a defining edge to the entry without blocking the light or view. "The floor-to-ceiling glass allows a seamless connection and gracious portal to the outdoors," says Pursley.

PAGE 108 An intimate dining area doubles as a library anchored by a tongue-and-groove oak table crafted entirely from remnant flooring panels. The ladder was made from an 18th-century roof truss.

PAGE 109 A contemporary credenza lends geometric earthiness to the rear entryway, where sliding glass doors lead to the backyard.

ABOVE A collection of lucite-framed prayer scripts hang over a streamlined bed outfitted in custom Perennials bedding.

RIGHT Roof overhangs shade both indoors and out from harsh sunlight, making for comfortable outdoor dining on the custom concrete-and-wood table.

Magnum Opus

◆◆◆

Amid the historic homes of Atlanta's Ansley Park, architect and designer
Bobby McAlpine creates an ode to sensual starkness and unapologetic design.

PAGE 114 McAlpine introduces wood and steel as darker elements with "graphic strength" adding a sense of compression to the lofty heights and airy whiteness. Kitchen barstools are from his McAlpine Home collection for Holland MacRae.

PAGE 115 McAlpine considers his home a "well-traveled vessel," a launching pad for creativity with a place for "everything that comes aboard," he says. Full of striking vignettes and forms, like this stairwell, "it needed to be vague in origin and time."

ABOVE Eschewing sweeping rooflines and idiosyncratic flourishes in favor of crisp lines, McAlpine experimented with stripped-down forms, sans traditional architectural elements "that trigger familiar emotions and obvious warm-and-fuzzy feelings," he says.

RIGHT In his light-drenched salon, McAlpine hangs antique lanterns constructed of vintage parts bought in France on custom trapezes. Klismos chairs surround an antique dining table, while terra-cotta lions stand guard by a Philippe Starck egg sculpture.

LEFT An oculus at the top of the stairwell sends cascades of light throughout the home, designed as a modern sanctuary of sorts, complete with a central axis and transept.

BELOW A wood and marble powder room subverts all norms, as an antique Venetian bird sculpture watches over washed hands.

LEFT The designer's home and studio, shared with his partner Blake Weeks, is a repository for fanciful objects of mesmerizing contrast that mirror the architect's own eclectic curiosity.

RIGHT A monochrome palette throughout the home, including this cloud-like bedroom, creates "a calming canvas that allows those in the house to have the floor," McAlpine says.

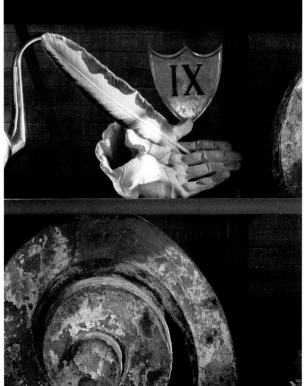

Graceland Redux

◆ ◆ ◆

In Music City, a classic white-columned manse becomes
a symphony of modern art and objet, thanks to
West Coast–based designer Richard Hallberg's hushed restraint.

LEFT "I wanted everything to feel cohesive, clean, and tied together. I don't like jarring transitions," says Hallberg, who carries forward hints of the exterior bluestone with hand-dipped Japanese rice paper squares on the entryway walls, running clear through to the library. Set against the undulant squares, everything appears artfully modern.

RIGHT In the dining room, Hallberg pares things down to simple elegance with extra servings of natural light. The carved wood chairs, chandelier, and table are by Dennis & Leen, one of Hallberg's enterprises.

RIGHT In the library, Hallberg curates layered vignettes. The overall effect feels "organic, calm, bright, casual, and incredibly interesting," the homeowner says.

PAGES 120-121 Hallberg recasts the former red brick exterior in piano key hues, with a chorus of sculpted boxwoods— a Southern hallmark— flanking the entryway.

LEFT Hallberg creates visual harmony by syncing the slick with the rustic, the precious piece with the found object. Chess, by John Cage (1968), hangs over a custom linen sofa.

BELOW A custom avian wall installation takes flight over a Parsons-style console and antique marble mortars.

> ❝ I wanted everything to feel cohesive, clean, and tied together. ❞

◇◇◇

RICHARD HALLBERG, DESIGNER

ABOVE Gentle melodies of ivory and gray hum along in the den (connected to the kitchen), where the designer allows space for silence to chime in as well.

RIGHT Raw, reclaimed beams from a Pennsylvania barn radiate a sense of history, counterbalancing the kitchen's glossy Belgian tile. The barstools are generously scaled reproductions of European antiques, cozied up to a mod waterfall island.

Wide Open Spaces

◆ ◆ ◆

In a historic Dallas neighborhood, designer
Meredith McBrearty and architect Ryan Street reprise the
suburban swagger of the American Midcentury.

PAGES 128-129 Douglas fir ceilings extend from the interior out, and Texas limestone lends a sculptural organic feel to columns and garden walls, examples of "natural materials utilized in a very sophisticated, modern way," says Street.

ABOVE Form and function meld seamlessly as McBrearty pairs a curvy oak console with a dining table inspired by a Japanese sword rest. A painting by Colombian American artist America Martin fills the dining room with guests.

LEFT Steel-framed glass and crisp, reticular lines give this home modernist flair, but inside, casual comfort rules. In the family room, a pop-art painting sums up the tone McBrearty had in mind: "informal, down to earth, and, most of all, fun!" The pool nestles close to the house and patio.

PAGES 132-133 A vaulted wood ceiling and stone wall add earthy texture to the living room, where McBrearty places lounge chairs and a sculptural 1960s French armchair around a handcrafted walnut-slab coffee table. The sofa's wooden arms are "wide enough to rest a drink on," the designer notes. "We loved that about it."

ABOVE A clean, simple aesthetic echoed by a palette of warm neutrals makes for a serene bedroom, where McBrearty adds depth with an artful wallcovering referencing the Southern California mountains.

RIGHT McBrearty's recipe for bathroom luxury: a sunken soaking tub, an outdoor garden shower, and loads of glorious light.

◆ CHAPTER 5 ◆

Artful and Bold

H OMES ARE SHELTER, havens of retreat and comfort. Our domestic realm is where we cook, eat, sleep, watch movies, fold laundry, play Scrabble with the kids, and cuddle with our pets, but our houses are also canvas, stage, and theater—for our guests and also for ourselves. Places where imagination and creativity can be showcased and nurtured. Here, under a familiar roof, amid the trappings of daily life, a playful sense of whimsy and wonder can be unleashed, a love of the quirky and offbeat, the abstract, surreal, or ultra-real expressed. Rooms, however stately or humble, are like clay to the sculptor or watercolor to the impressionist. They can be transformed by color, form, texture, light, and drama, and by works of art itself.

In this respect, Southern homes are no different than homes anywhere—from the prehistoric caves of Bhimbetka, to the finest castles in Europe, to the humble cottage down the street. Art enlivens them, and the designers and homeowners included in this chapter celebrate this. Thanks to boisterous strokes of magenta, yellow, and cobalt blue, old Southern living rooms once again enthrall; floors checkerboarded in black and white marble announce game on. As Texas-based designer and art collector Todd Romano says of his "wackadoodle combinations" and admittedly "insane" color choices, "it's meant to be provocative and non-serious and fun."

In Palm Beach, consummate artist of interiors Bunny Williams dabbles in pink plaster (among other hues), painting bedroom walls the color of seashells. South Carolina–based designer Angie Hranowsky fearlessly collages layers of fun and funky, glazed with posh sophistication, for clients in Austin, Texas, while Melanie Turner and architect Yong Pak invoke art to temper the formality of a grand Mediterranean Revival in Atlanta. From miniscule details to flamboyant gestures, art brings extra spark to homes steeped in the South's heat, in a most refreshing way. If a dining room cum-modern art gallery means getting to dine every night with Roy Lichtenstein, why not?

LEFT A French blue study summons safari instincts, thanks to tiger-striped stools and a collection of vintage animal prints.

PAGES 136-137 Modern art abounds in this living room by designer Angie Hranowsky, where glossy daffodil walls and deep plum accents spark up creative juices.

Austin Powered

◆ ◆ ◆

Designer Angie Hranowsky lights up a
late 20th-century Tudor with vanguard shades
of yellow, saffron, peach, and fuchsia.

RIGHT Spicy red drapes complement a high-gloss French blue in a not-too-studious study, where Hranowsky playfully mixes in animal prints and funky lighting.

PAGES 140-141 "Classic but cool" is Charleston-based Hranowsky's vibe for this Austin, Texas, home, where pickled floors, new steel casement doors and sunny hues amplify the natural light.

ABOVE In a living room vignette, vintage spoon-back chairs flank a settee covered in a brush-stroke-inspired linen, so even the furniture feels like an art project.

RIGHT A painting by Colombian American artist America Martin marks a chic point of entry in a breezeway linking the main residence to a pool house.

❝ I wanted to walk that line between edginess and timelessness. ❞

◇◇◇

ANGIE HRANOWSKY, DESIGNER

ABOVE A deeply tufted emerald banquette and saturated aubergine sconce shades make a corner of the dining room feel like a hip supper club.

LEFT Glossy sage, antiqued silver-leaf panels, and regal violet form a dynamic canvas for a vintage brown hexagonal table and klismos-style chairs. "I want my rooms to feel natural, not formulaic," says Hranowsky.

LEFT Look closely—the design for this zippy zigzag wallpaper is actually a bevy of moths, which the owner dubs her "barflies," adding winged wonder to the bar.

ABOVE Taking full advantage of dormer angles, Hranowsky encases a guest room in a Matisse-inspired tree pattern, creating a black-and-white woodland fantasy.

RIGHT Hranowsky can afford to color outside the lines, so to speak, because she also embraces the tidy linear beauty of midcentury design, as with this custom-tailored bed and similarly sleek settee.

French Deco Decadence

◆ ◆ ◆

A century-old Atlanta home reclaims the élan of its youth with
ravishing neutrals, art-steeped salons, and sophisticated poise.

LEFT "It's about fresh takes on classical design elements," says designer Melanie Turner. She tempers the living room's gold-and-silver-hued formality with art, including two mixed-media works by artist Todd Murphy, who incorporated remnant swatches of the home's original wallpaper in his ball-gown creations.

RIGHT The wife calls the brass-accented butler's pantry her "dirty kitchen," but here it's more like a floral designer's haven.

BELOW The dining room, part of a larger salon that opens to a solarium/bar, is animated by jazzy fabric and hand-painted French Empire–style credenzas. Turner freely mixes period pieces, combining parquet de Versailles flooring with a Deco-esque goatskin-covered dining table. "The feel is elevated but relaxed, almost like you're on vacation," she says.

PAGE 148 The study, embraced by white oak and leather paneling, showcases a quartet of Jenga series abstracts flanking a Roman-inspired mirror. Toffee-hued Christopher Spitzmiller lamps make handsome reading lights.

PAGE 149 Turner loved the playful "domino effect" of these black and white marble tiles with contrasting circles, from which rises a gracefully pirouetting staircase with a handcrafted wrought-iron balustrade.

> **❝** The unexpected details we put in the house pay homage to classicism and traditional homes. But they're quirky or have a bit of a twist. **❞**

◇◇◇

MELANIE TURNER, DESIGNER

ABOVE Sunny Atlanta breakfast nook or swanky Parisian cafe? Hard to tell, thanks to a custom banquette hugging the arched window and Serena & Lily bistro chairs.

RIGHT Tiled arcs put a chic spin on the traditional barrel-vaulted ceiling, while encaustic cement tile floors give the kitchen a French bistro flavor.

RIGHT While the main living and entertaining areas are dominated by neutrals, Turner changed things up in the bedrooms, giving each one a different palette. Here soft lavender and lilac enchant the daughter's dreams.

ABOVE A mod 1960s bentwood divider by Ludvík Volák adds groovy beech gridwork to a basement media room, where a mercury glass fireplace surround adds another artful element.

RIGHT Turner ignites full Deco glam in this powder room, where sheeny black and gold bows to fabulously glitzy lighting.

San Antonio Salon

• • •

Returning to his Texas roots, designer
Todd Romano finds his dream house—a repository
for his epic pursuit of the art uncommon.

LEFT Vintage silver-leaf wallpaper gives Romano's dining room a mercurial sense of movement, creating a shimmering backdrop for works by Roy Lichtenstein, George N. Morris, Josef Albers, and Robert Goodnough.

RIGHT Romano embraces intense color and "wacka-doodle combinations," he says, "precisely because I didn't want the place to look like my grandmother's house."

RIGHT Romano loves the tension of slightly off-kilter combinations, pairing an ornate Chinese Chippendale-style mirror with a Louis XVI mahogany-and-marble commode.

PAGES 156-157 The library is a study in contrasting textures, as Romano layers ultrasuede seating, fur and sisal rugs against eggplant-hued glazed lacquer walls.

" I freely admit that the colors are kind of insane, but it's meant to be provocative and nonserious and fun. At the end of the day, it's all just a frame for your life. "

◇◇◇

TODD ROMANO, DESIGNER AND HOMEOWNER

LEFT Graphic punch spices up Romano's sleek kitchen, thanks to custom Talavera tiles arranged in a chevron pattern and glossy ebony cabinetry.

RIGHT Cheerful awning stripes above and big black-and-white checks below sandwich a delightful sunroom, complete with Napoleon III lounge chairs and a chaise-style sofa. "The last thing I'd ever want is for any place of mine to feel stuffy," Romano says.

RIGHT Bubblegum pink glosses the interior of a breakfast room china cabinet, where Romano showcases his collection of Portuguese and Italian cabbageware.

PAGES 162-163 Art, books, and Peruvian and Spanish Colonial mirrors parade against red wool felt walls in Romano's bedroom, where a velvet Louis XV–style step stool serves as decadent doggie steps.

Villa Va-voom

∙ ∙ ∙

From seashell pinks to garden greens,
Bunny Williams's artful refresh of a
Palm Beach Mediterranean-style villa
celebrates a tropical palette.

PAGES 164-165 In addition to adding a guest wing to the villa, the pool and landscaping were totally redone, evoking 1920s Palm Beach glamour.

ABOVE Williams aimed for a "forever look," but one that wasn't dusty or dated. Eighteenth-century Italian antiques, like this exquisitely painted chair, fit the villa's vernacular. Living room walls in a muted ivory embellish the molding and showcase the owner's vibrant art.

LEFT Looking outside at surrounding foliage, Williams garnered inspiration for the living room's acid-green palette. "When you do just one color, it's less busy," she says.

LEFT It's hard not to have a good day when breakfast starts in Williams's happy homage to pink, punctuated by a custom geometric rug. A vintage Murano chandelier and 18th-century Italian commode add regal elements.

RIGHT Williams serves up art at every turn, with custom Venetian plaster walls, a painted sisal rug, and contemporary resin-topped table juxtaposed with an 18th-century Italian console and more modern art.

LEFT Bougainvillea crown the loggia's Italianate arches, hinting at the bursting garden of colors inside the home.

BELOW A marble dolphin fountain cascades into the hot tub, nestled privately in lush tropical greenery.

LEFT A guesthouse living room is family movie-night central, with plenty of stylish seating and a spunky modern take on Mediterranean-tile walls, custom created by digital printing.

PAGES 172-173 "When I think of Florida, I think of seashells," says Williams, who draped a John Robshaw bed in silvery-pink fabric that "echoes the sheen of the inside of a shell. Pink is such a great color. I used to avoid it, but now it's my favorite." The glossy gray ceiling reflects light to make the room feel larger.

◆ CHAPTER 6 ◆

Classic Revivals

P ATINAED SURFACES. BIG OLD COLUMNS, sturdy despite their age, or because of it. A beloved farmhouse passed down for generations. Time works a strange sort of magic in the South, where the palimpsest of centuries is palpable as old homes are revered and revived. Antebellum or turn-of-the-century, classic homes tell stories with walls and cornices and weathered sash windows bearing witness to the scars and beauty of the past. They are the beloved elders of the built environment, and we Southerners (for better or worse) do tend to worship our ancestors.

To love and revive an older home takes devotion and, yes, resources. Sometimes it even entails sawing a cottage in half to gingerly move it 65 miles across Georgia, as designer Furlow Gatewood did. But the care and love given is more than returned, as is evident in the houses featured here. Classic, however, need not always mean old, as architect James F. Carter proves in his newly constructed "old house" in Birmingham, an ode to proportion, scale, and enduring materials. In Palm Beach, designer Susan Zises Green revels in the intricate details of a palatial Italian Romanesque, while a humble railroad cottage in the Arkansas Delta, a farming family home for four generations, shines after Heather Chadduck gives it equal TLC. In Beaufort, South Carolina, designer Elizabeth Locke takes on a former Union Army hospital, complete with its own ghost, where she lets the alchemy of age be beauty enough.

The classic homes of the South continue to enchant simply because they speak to the timelessness of great design and its relevance for contemporary living. Sixteen-foot ceilings will never go out of style, nor will the charm of a wraparound porch or allure of gothic detail. Houses built with such care "deserve to have their history show," says Zises Green. And when it sparkles thanks to thoughtful, visionary designers and history-loving homeowners, well, even better.

LEFT Architect James Carter gave his Mountain Brook home an air of "easy grace," designing rooms with old-school scale and detail, like this library paneled in antiqued oak.

PAGES 174-175 A timeless mix of antiques and books creates an elegant landing in architect and designer James F. Carter's Birmingham home.

Old Soul

◆ ◆ ◆

Birmingham architect James F. Carter imbues
new construction with old character, building himself
a "forever house" filled with cherished collections.

PAGE 178 Details like a marble-surround fireplace in the owner's bedroom give old flavor to the new house, with an antique Regency side chair, stool, and vintage sconces adding to the timeworn feel.

PAGE 179 Whitewashed brick with gray shutters and a reclaimed slate roof give the home a stately, established feel. Carter wanted it to fit quietly into the neighborhood. "It's not 'Oh, look at me, I'm so special,'" he says.

LEFT A handsome stairwell curls toward a traditional black and white landing, but not without including room for books. "They give warmth and visual appeal. And anyway, I'm a book fiend," the architect confesses.

RIGHT In the octagonal dining room, built-in bookshelves and plainspoken bare floors lend rustic charm to fine antique furnishings. Carter almost painted the walls a lacquered orange, but he was glad his decorator friend Jane Hawkins Hoke talked him into a subdued apricot. "I wanted bold but not cartoonish," he says.

LEFT Golden accents and floral fabrics make a charming corner for Carter's antiques, including this French desk and side table in a guest bedroom.

RIGHT A four-poster bed that belonged to his grandparents is one of Carter's most-prized pieces, with canopy and bed skirt in a Jane Shelton fabric.

LEFT French doors leading to the back garden are guarded by a pair of gilded William Kent eagle consoles—a Carter must-have. "Almost every magazine page I tore out featured rooms with eagle consoles," he says.

> ❝ I wanted the house to be a bit rambling. I wanted quirks. I wanted personality. ❞

JAMES F. CARTER, ARCHITECT AND HOMEOWNER

ABOVE In an upstairs hallway, Carter tastefully employs elements—wainscoting, classic stripes, and an antique rug on wide-plank floors—that are as equally at home in the 18th century as the 21st.

RIGHT The owner's bedroom, tucked under a slanting roof, is painted a rich green, a hue Carter describes as "strong and cozy." Built-in bookshelves look like an old doorway closed off and filled in over time.

Enduring Opulance

• • •

Designer Susan Zises Green updates a
fabled 1920s Palm Beach mansion, preserving its
authentic detail while ushering in the sun.

LEFT Iconic flourishes of this Maurice Fatio (famed architect to the Rockefellers and Vanderbilts) mansion remained intact, including the entryway's 1920s curlicue pendant and hand-carved ceiling, giving the New York–based designer an ornate canvas.

RIGHT To cozy-up the home's vastness, including a generous living room, Zises Green carved out intimate conversation areas, bathed in genteel pinks and cream. "My goal was to lighten and brighten," she says, "and create a joyous environment in which to live."

RIGHT Magnificent hand-carved and painted ceilings are a signature of this Italian Romanesque home. While celebrating their elaborateness, Zises Green softens their heft with lighter, more modern touches.

PAGES 184-185 The living room's four seating groups are grounded by one custom-woven rug. Zises Green chose simple curtains to allow the arched windows speak for themselves. Mantel and chandelier are original.

RIGHT The dining room, with original chandelier, is enveloped in Venetian plaster in a custom shade that Zises Green calls "lettuce green." The armchairs and velvet-covered side chairs are all antique.

LEFT White, chrome, and copper play well together in a spacious kitchen, complete with pizza oven, that manages to feel both vintage and vogue.

RIGHT Dreamy pale blues give soft, fresh romance to this airy guest bedroom.

LEFT Extending off the living room, the loggia offers relaxed outdoor entertaining and living space, with salmon-hued slipper chairs along with vintage rattan.

ABOVE A patterned pool bottom adds splashy dynamism to the palm-studded garden.

Georgia Gothic Glory

◆ ◆ ◆

Decorator and antiques devotee Furlow
Gatewood rescued a derelict old cottage in a rural
Georgia town, and loved it back to life.

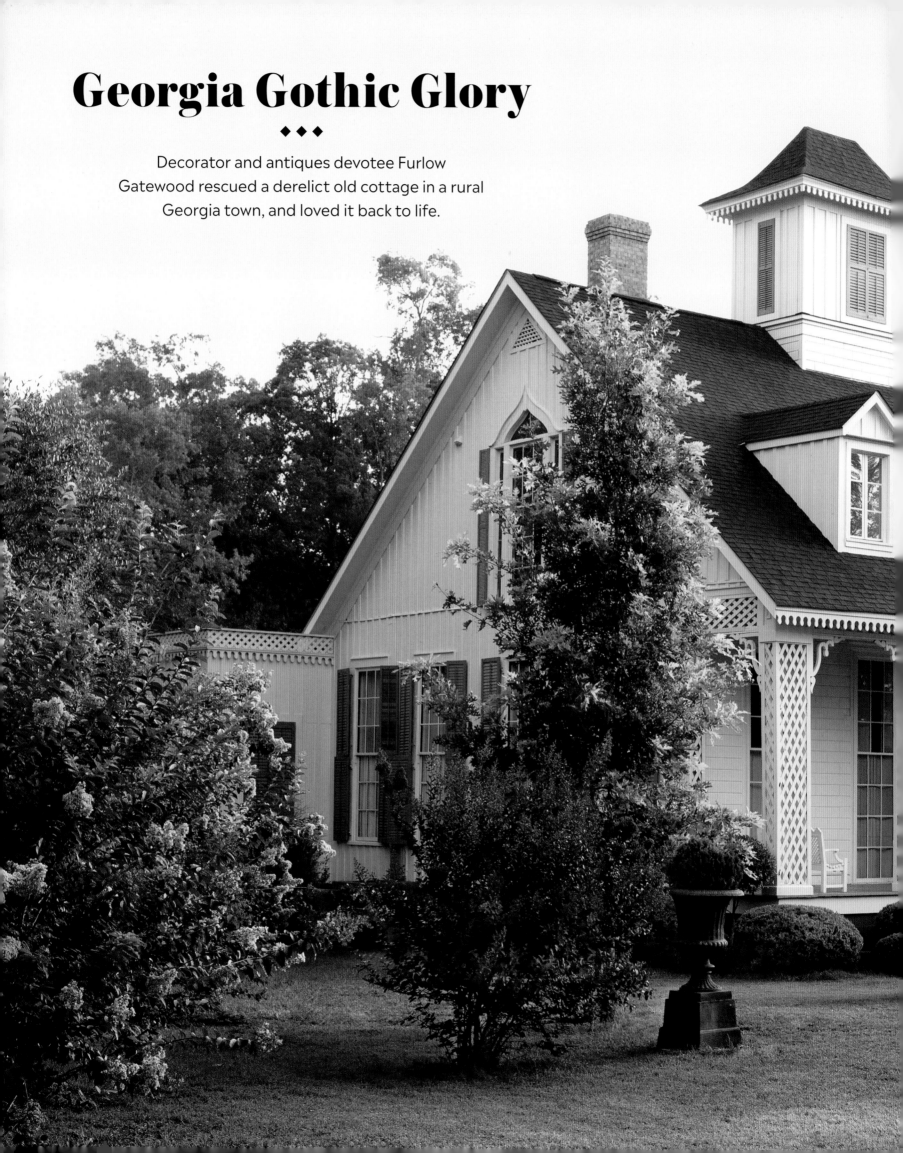

RIGHT Because no
Southern cottage is
complete without a porch,
Gatewood added this
airy trellised haven
furnished in a throwaway
mix of wicker, happy ikats,
and batiks. The floor?
Painted gray, naturally.

BELOW Classics upon
classic, a Diana of the Hunt
goddess presides over
the light-filled entry hall,
where Gatewood used
beveled wood to replicate
the "rusticated" faux
stone exterior.

ABOVE In the dining room,
blue and white porcelain and
gilt mirrors punch up the
handsome gray. Gatewood
painted the floor in gray
and white blocks in lieu of
a rug. "More dog-friendly,"
says the ever-practical
designer. Feathery tole
leaf ornaments, crafted in
India, are his design.

PAGES 192-193 Smitten by
loads of 19th-century
charm—dormers, a wide
front porch, bric-a-brac
embellishment, 16-foot
ceilings—Gatewood knew
good bones when he
saw it. He had the cottage
cut in half in order
to move it 65 miles to
Americus, Georgia.

LEFT Gatewood makes guests feel extra cozy with old-fashioned touches like an antique canopy bed, a vintage rug and an old needlepoint artwork.

ABOVE Gatewood admits his appetite for antiques is not easily sated. He collects, and collects some more, and arranges his finds with grace and ease, as with this bedroom chest and Anglo-Indian campaign chair.

PAGES 198-199 A gray and white color scheme is "very cooling," says Gatewood, whose adept use of symmetry brings order to his array of treasures, including a collection of Chinese porcelain birds.

ABOVE A delightful green belvedere (matching the cottage shutters) makes a quaint roosting spot for Gatewood's 40 peacocks.

RIGHT An allée of blue hydrangeas heralds a beautiful Southern welcome on the approach to Gatewood's compound.

Beaufort Belle

◆◆◆

Beneath a canopy of oaks beside a
South Carolina salt marsh, an enchanting 1859 home
in full columned grandeur lures jewelry
designer Elizabeth Locke to the Low Country.

LEFT Age shows its beauty on timeworn columns. The grand porch is ideal for all-season entertaining in Beaufort's temperate climate.

PAGE 204-205 A 19th-century beauty in Beaufort, South Carolina, retains its centuries-old élan.

ABOVE Jewelry designer Locke remembers the first time she entered the empty home: "My heart skipped a beat." She was wowed by the spectacular symmetry of the double staircase and other original, intact elements of the light-filled house.

LEFT Years take their toll, but the intricate jib windows that double as doors from living room to porch, and provide natural air conditioning, are still in working order. The home's 23 rooms include 79 original windows.

RIGHT To honor the home's unadorned elegance, Locke resolved to decorate only as absolutely necessary. "No rugs, no big curtains, very spare," she says.

BELOW Original handmade bricks in a geometric design anchor the ground floor, an area that would have been used mostly for utilitarian purposes.

RIGHT A simple antique sleigh bed welcomes guests in one of the many guest bedrooms.

Family Affair

◆ ◆ ◆

In a tiny railroad town in the Arkansas Delta (population 200),
a farmhouse passed down through generations gets a refresh
from Birmingham-based designer Heather Chadduck.

PAGE 210 Young newlyweds moving into the husband's fourth-generation family homestead wanted to honor the home's lineage while infusing fresh personality. Chadduck began with a uniform coat of Alabaster white paint, layering in color and statement lighting. "When I first visited the Delta, it was growing season. The vivid greens, dark browns, and harvest yellows in the fields were my design compass," says Chadduck, who chose Jasper Malmaison sofa fabric as her "jumping-off point."

PAGE 211 Off the kitchen, an enclosed dogtrot becomes a mudroom-slash-coffee spot, with a sunny banquette and vintage round glass-top table.

LEFT "The smallest room in the house is the one we live in most," says the wife of the cozy breakfast/sitting room, where a wall of built-ins provides crucial storage for the small three-bedroom cottage. "I was shopping for cabinet hardware, and my father-in-law, who has a great design eye, says, 'Oh I have some,' and brings me a toolbox of beautiful brass knobs," she adds.

ABOVE Tortoise shell wallpaper by Schumacher and antiqued gold shelving transform a tiny alcove into a tony bar.

RIGHT In a hallway where the husband's sister once slept in a crib, an antique buffet stores linens. The maple flooring throughout is original, but needed restoring. In the process of pulling up old planks, they discovered they were all stamped with the husband's great-grandfather's name.

ABOVE A tiny study with loads of light and heirloom pieces like the cane back chairs has become the couple's favorite hangout spot.

RIGHT "Wallcoverings breathe life into rooms like these with their 11-foot-tall ceilings," says Chadduck, who chose a dramatic linear stripe for the dining room. "Situated in the hub of the house, the room needed a neutral palette," she says. A pair of shell-topped china cabinets are original to the house, as is the chandelier.

" I was immediately charmed by the home's patina. It feels entirely rooted in history. "

◇◇◇

HEATHER CHADDUCK, DESIGNER

LEFT A time-capsule guest bedroom features twin beds that the husband slept in as a boy, and his father before him. "That kind of history you can't really erase," says the wife, who also kept the room's original wallpaper, which Chadduck had repaired and restored.

ABOVE Chadduck turned an extra living room into the owners' bedroom, "since it had a fireplace and lots of windows," and felt like an appropriate amendment to the floor plan, she says. Sisal rugs are her go-to to anchor dark wood antiques.

INDEX

PHOTOGRAPHY CREDITS

William Abranowicz 46-53, 104-112

Melanie Acevedo 72-83

Mali Azima back cover, 148-155

Emily Followill cover, 34-45

Douglass Friedman 128-135, 156-163

J. Savage Gibson 54-61

Laurey W. Glenn 20-23

Allison Gootee 8, 100-103, 210-217

Noel Hunt, 223 (top)

Maximillian Kim-Bee 120-127, 194-203

Francesco Lagnese 2-3, 6, 164-173, 186-193

Thomas Loof 24-27

Julia Lynn 136-147

James Merrell 92-99, 204-209

Amy Nuensinger 28-33

Mimi Read 62-65

Annie Schlechter 174-185

Simon Upton 114-119

Brie Williams 1, 84-91, 113

Brian Woodcock 4, 10-19, 66-71, 223 (bottom)

STEPHANIE HUNT is a writer in Charleston, South Carolina, and regular contributor to Veranda. A native Southerner, she writes about style and design and community and culture for a number of publications, including *Coastal Living, Southern Living, LUXE, The Washington Post,* and *Charleston Magazine.*

STEELE THOMAS MARCOUX is the editor of *Veranda* and a veteran of the design publishing industry, having served in senior editorial roles at *Country Living, Coastal Living,* and *Southern Living.* She serves on the board of directors for the Alabama School of Fine Arts in Birmingham, Alabama, where she lives with her husband, two sons, and dog.

Copyright 2022 by
Hearst Magazine Media, Inc.

All rights reserved. The written
instructions in this volume are intended
for the personal use of the reader and
may be reproduced for that purpose only.
Any other use, especially commercial use,
is forbidden under law without the written
permission of the copyright holder

Cover and book design by Erynn Hassinger

Library of Congress Cataloging-in-
Publication Data Available on Request

10 9 8 7 6 5 4 3 2 1

Published by Hearst Home, an imprint of
Hearst Books/Hearst Communications, Inc.

Hearst Magazine Media, Inc.

300 West 57th Street
New York, New York 10019

Veranda, Hearst Home, the Hearst Home
logo, and Hearst Books are registered
trademarks of Hearst Communications, Inc.

For information about custom editions,
special sales, premium and corporate
purchases: hearst.com/magazines/
hearst-books

Printed in China

ISBN 978-1-950785-80-3